Tatted Lace Accessories

Donatella Ciotti

SEARCH PRESS

Dedicated to my husband Massimo

A big 'Thank you' to Viviana Reverso, Elena Turconi and the photographer Giorgio Uccellini

First published in Great Britain in 2015
by Search Press Limited, Wellwood,
North Farm Road, Tunbridge Wells, Kent TN2 3DR

First published in Italy by Il Castello Collane Tecniche, Milano
Original Italian title: *Pizzo Chiacchierino.*

Copyright © 2014 Il Castello srl
Via Milano 73/75 - 20010, Cornaredo (Milano), Italy

Translation by Burravoe Translation Services

Typesetting by Greengate Publishing Services,
Tonbridge, Kent

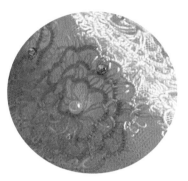

ISBN: 978-1-78221-229-4

The Publishers and author can accept no responsibility for any consequences arising from the information,
advice or instructions given in this publication.

Readers are permitted to reproduce any of the items in this book for their personal use, or for the
purposes of selling for charity, free of charge and without the prior permission of the Publishers. Any use
of the items for commercial purposes is not permitted without the prior permission of the Publishers.

Printed in China

Contents

Introduction   page 4
Tools   page 6
Threads and accessories   page 8

TECHNIQUES   page 10

Half stitch – A   page 12
Half stitch – B   page 12
Josephine knot   page 13
Double stitch or double knot   page 13
Double stitches with picots   page 14
Simple ring   page 16
Ring with picots   page 16
Closing knots   page 17
Chains   page 17
Joining motifs   page 18
Unpicking the work   page 19
When the thread breaks   page 19
Hiding the loose ends   page 20
Working with beads   page 21

PROJECTS   page 22

Two-tone bracelet   page 24
Spiral necklace   page 26
Rose place holders   page 28
Circle bracelet   page 30
Bracelet with beads   page 34
Interwoven bracelet   page 38
Daisy bracelet   page 40
Square earrings with swarovski crystals   page 44
Flower earrings   page 48
Four-leaf clover bracelet   page 52
Necklace and earrings with roses   page 56
Purse and mobile phone pouch   page 60
Necklace and earrings with ring motif   page 66
Lilac earrings   page 68
Grey necklace   page 70
Blue earrings   page 71
Clover necklace   page 72
Purple and fuchsia collar   page 76
Beaded favours   page 78
Sachets with poinsettias   page 82
Flowers   page 88
Black choker   page 90

Introduction

Tatted lace has been back in vogue for a few years now. Its enchanting delicacy is truly stunning and, unsuprisingly, has become a feature in high fashion. Follow my step-by-step techniques and I will show you how to make this exquisite lace for yourself.

Rest assured that this type of handwork is simple and does not require a lot of concentration. It's also very compact and, whether you use the traditional shuttle or a needle, it's easy to carry around and work on anywhere.

You can use the same tatting patterns for the needle technique as for shuttle tatting, however, in this book, I will focus on tatting with a needle, as it is a newer technique – although one that has been a traditional craft for centuries in the Middle East.

The needle technique is quicker to learn than the shuttle and has the added benefit that you can unravel it if you make a mistake (anyone who works with a shuttle will know that once the ring is closed, it is impossible to unpick it).

Many materials can be used, from very fine thread to cord, along with beads of different types and sizes. Although the stitches may not be as tight as they would be if they were made with a shuttle, with the right needle (one that is thinner than the thread) and ensuring you pull the stitches tight, the results can be fantastic.

The designs I will share with you here are beautiful and include lovely bracelets, earrings, necklaces and brooches. Each project is illustrated and explained with step-by-step instructions. There are also diagrams to help you make, and even invent, new pieces yourself.

Hopefully, these designs will inspire you with ideas for special occasions. Tatted lace makes perfect accessories for weddings or christenings; as well as decorations for tables, purses, mobile phone holders and much more.

Best wishes and happy tatting to you all!

Donatella Ciotti

Tools

Needles: You can use all long needles for this work, preferably those with rounded tips. The eye should not be wider than the needle itself. A large eye enlarges the stitches and leaves them loose.

The size of the needle depends on the gauge (thickness) of the thread that is used.

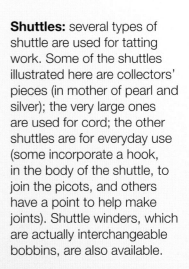

Shuttles: several types of shuttle are used for tatting work. Some of the shuttles illustrated here are collectors' pieces (in mother of pearl and silver); the very large ones are used for cord; the other shuttles are for everyday use (some incorporate a hook, in the body of the shuttle, to join the picots, and others have a point to help make joints). Shuttle winders, which are actually interchangeable bobbins, are also available.

Threads and accessories

Threads: all types of thread, including metallic thread, embroidery thread, cord, twine and linen thread can be used for tatting. It is however important that they are not too tightly twisted, otherwise they can curl up and get knotted when the thread is being let out. Experiment to find the thread best suited to your project.

NB: most of the generic threads listed for the projects in this book can be found from suppliers such as DMC and Anchor embroidery threads.

Assorted accessories:
beads, hooks and clasps.

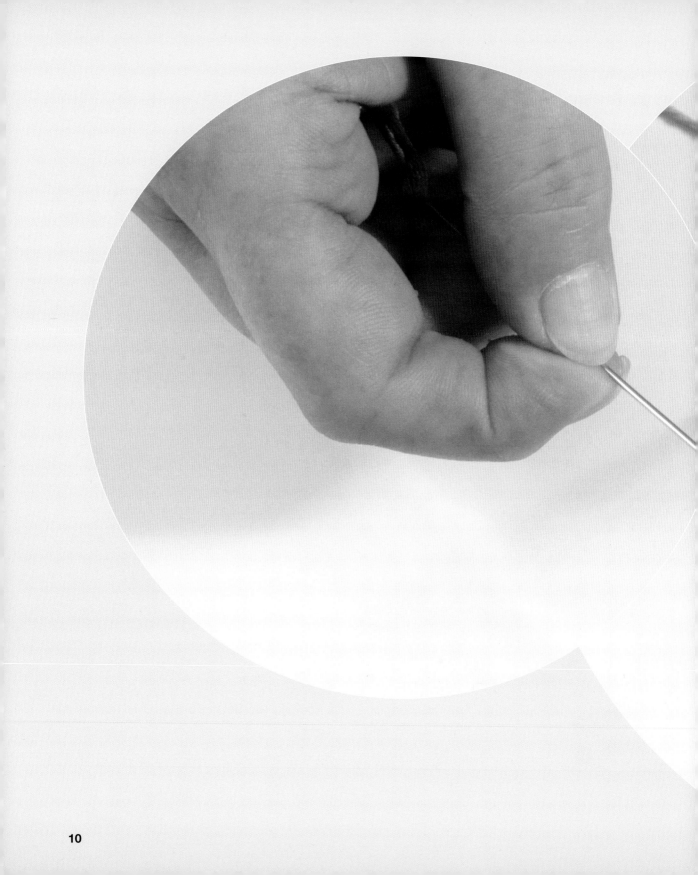

Techniques

HALF STITCH – A

1 Thread the needle without cutting the thread off the ball, leaving about 50cm (20in) on the side. From now on, this thread will be called the *carrier thread*. With your right index finger and thumb, hold the thread and needle together.

2–3 Wrap the thread from the ball around your left index finger. Loop it over the needle to make a knot and hold it down on the needle with your right index finger. Repeat the two steps described above and when you have finished, pull the needle through the stitches in such a way that the loose thread fills in the space that the needle occupied while you were tying the stitches, acting as a carrier thread.

HALF STITCH – B

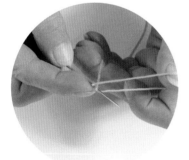

1 Thread the needle as explained above and wind the thread around your left thumb, inverting the position of the thread.

2–3 This way, the tip of the needle is between the index and middle fingers. Make a few more stitches, then pass the needle through them and pull it through.

JOSEPHINE KNOT

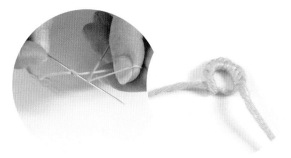

1–2 This is made up of a series of A or B half stitches. Pass the needle through the stitches, pull the thread to make a ring and tie a knot. This can be used as a decorative knot or as a closing loop on jewellery.

DOUBLE STITCH OR DOUBLE KNOT

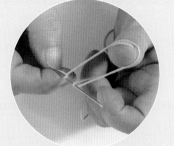

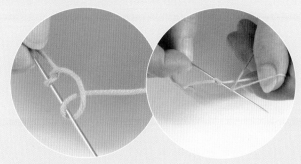

1 This is a combination of one A half stitch and one B half stitch. Hold the needle and the thread with the index finger and thumb, leaving a thread end about 50cm (20in) long and, with the thread coming from the ball, make the first half stitch.

2–3 With your index finger, firmly hold down the first half stitch and make the second one. Bring the second half knot close to the first, tighten them both, keeping them close and make a series of these stitches keeping them close together. At the end, pull the carrier thread on the needle through the stitches and out at the other end.

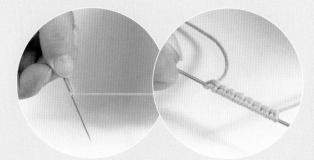

4–5 Start another series of stitches without leaving any space between the completed work and the new stitches. Continue in this way according to the instructions. This is the basic tatting stitch. Make sure the tension is the same for all the stitches so that the work looks even.

DOUBLE STITCHES WITH PICOTS

1 Thread the needle leaving a length of about 30cm (12in) to one side of the needle. Make 3 double stitches (as explained previously) keeping them close together.

2–3 At a distance of 5mm (¼in) from the last knot, make another series of double stitches. Continue this sequence alternating close stitches and distanced stitches.

4 Push all the stitches up close on the needle: now you have a series of picots alternating with groups of double stitches.

5 Pull the needle, passing the carrier thread through the stitches.

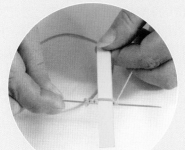

6 Picots can be small, medium or large sized. Small picots are usually used to make joins in the work or to make links, while the medium-sized and large ones are used as ornamentation. Until you gain more experience, you can use a piece of cardboard spacer as a gauge for the distances between stitches.

7 Prepare two strips of cardboard 1cm (⅜in) and 2cm (¾in) wide (or any other measurement you require). Make 3 double stitches, position the narrow cardboard strip on the needle, hold it in place with your right index finger and make three more double stitches. Then slide out the cardboard.

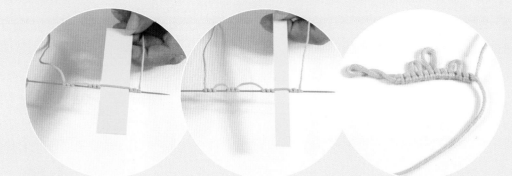

8–9–10 Likewise, make another picot with the wider cardboard strip. Repeat the steps as above with 3 double stitches, and make another picot with the narrow strip. Once again, make 3 double stitches, slide out the cardboard and pull the stitches up close to compact.

11 After pulling the needle through the stitches, pass it through the loop that forms at the end where you tied the first stitch. Close the ring by pulling the carrier thread.

SIMPLE RING

Tatting is a combination of knots or stitches worked over a thread, which, when pulled together, forms the characteristic rings, chains and picots.

1 To make a ring, leave about 50cm (20in) of thread in the eye of the needle and make 12 double stitches.

2 Pull the needle and thread through the stitches, leaving a small loop at the end.

3–4 Pass the needle through this end loop and pull the thread firmly. You have now formed the first ring.

RING WITH PICOTS

1 While working tatting designs, we often use rings with picots. If the picots are used to join several parts, they are small and barely visible. Make a series of double stitches and picots.

2 Make 20 double stitches making a small picot every 5 stitches, for a total of 3 picots. Pass the needle and thread through the stitches and pull the thread, thus closing the ring.

CLOSING KNOTS

CHAINS

1 Single knot: this should be made at the end of a circle or chain. It should lie flat while tying so that the work does not get twisted.

1 Position the needle close to the ring closure and make a double knot on the needle. Tighten the thread well and make 2 more double knots and a picot. This makes the first group of double stitches.

2 Repeat these steps three more times and end with 3 double stitches. Pass the carrier thread through the work with the needle, pull to form picots and compact the stitches. Now you have a chain or an arch.

3 Sometimes the chain needs to stay open, so after step 2, end with a single knot.

2–3 Double knot: made at the end of the work to finish it. First make a single knot, then pass the thread twice through the loop. Pull both threads to close. Thread the two ends, one by one, through a few stitches in the work and cut off the excess thread.

4–5 To join the chain end, pass the needle through the first picot after the end of the chain on the base ring, form a loop, by pulling the spool thread out of the picot using the needle tip. Pass the needle through this loop and pull and tighten to attach the chain. You have made a petal.

JOINING MOTIFS

To join a finished motif with another one that you are making, you can use a crochet hook. Make any motif to start with, for example, a flower with five petals.

1 Start by first making a central ring made up of groups of 4 double stitches and 3 small picots, then close the ring. Make the first chain of 5 double stitches, 1 picot and 5 more double stitches. Pull the needle and thread through the stitches and tie it with a single knot. You have made the first closed chain. Make another one in the same way.

2–3 Make the third chain. Make 5 double stitches, insert the crochet hook in the picot of the flower with 5 petals (see photo above) and pull out a small loop. Pass the needle through the loop and make 5 more double stitches. Attach the chain to the central ring.

4–5 Make the last chain (or petal, depending upon what you are making) and then take the needle out from the wrong side of the work. Cut the thread from the spool and tie off the ends. Slip the thread ends inside the work and cut off the excess thread.

UNPICKING THE WORK

You may occasionally happen to make a mistake or a wrong stitch. This would spoil the look of the work, so you will need to undo it and correct the mistake. If the work is still on the needle, it will be easy to identify and correct the mistake, but if you have gone ahead and inserted the carrier thread, you just need to loosen the knots and slip them off the thread. Unthread the needle and with its point, slip the carrier thread out from its insertion point.

WHEN THE THREAD BREAKS

1–2–3 Sometimes during tatting the thread can break or prove to be too short for your work. This means you need to add another thread. However, you can do this only at the end of a ring or at the beginning of a chain, otherwise the knot will make it hard to continue with the work.

Make a slip knot with the new thread and slip it over the old thread. Pull the thread and tighten. Holding the old thread, slide the knot to its base, touching the end of the work. From now on you will work with the new thread. When you have finished the motif, apply a drop of clear nail varnish to the slip knot and cut off the excess thread.

4 You can also join the new thread by knotting it with the old one, using a single knot and then a double knot, very close to the work, making sure it is at the end of a ring or chain.

HIDING THE LOOSE ENDS

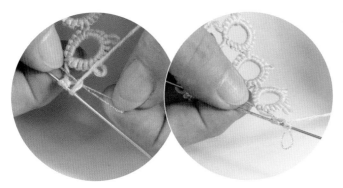 

1–2 After you have made all the knots to tie off the loose ends, you will need to hide the loose threads to prevent them looking unattractive on the back of the work. This is particularly the case with pieces that can also be seen from the back, such as earrings. To solve this problem, take a very thin thread in a contrasting colour and make two open loops and use them as follows: at the beginning of the work, position the contrasting thread along the needle, folded in half with the loop facing the eye of the needle. At the start, hold it down firmly with your fingers, make a couple of stitches, and then leave it free but do not pull it out. Continue with the work (this additional thread will not affect the work).

3 When you are nearing the end of the ring or chain, position a second contrasting thread on the needle, this time with the loop facing the point of the needle, and work it in using the same procedure as before.

4 Once you have finished the motif, tie it off with a closing knot and cut the thread; insert one of the two ends inside the loop of contrasting thread. Then pull the extra thread out from between the stitches. Repeat with the other loop. This will help you finish the work. It should now look perfect. Cut off the extra thread when you have finished.

WORKING WITH BEADS

1 Small and large beads, sequins and many other accessories can be used in needle tatting to make jewellery. Before you start working, thread the items that you need for your project onto the working thread. If your pattern calls for several different accessories, thread them in the required sequence.

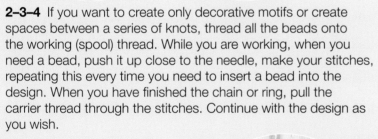

2–3–4 If you want to create only decorative motifs or create spaces between a series of knots, thread all the beads onto the working (spool) thread. While you are working, when you need a bead, push it up close to the needle, make your stitches, repeating this every time you need to insert a bead into the design. When you have finished the chain or ring, pull the carrier thread through the stitches. Continue with the design as you wish.

5–6 Using the same technique, you can make picots with beads on them.

Projects

Two-tone bracelet

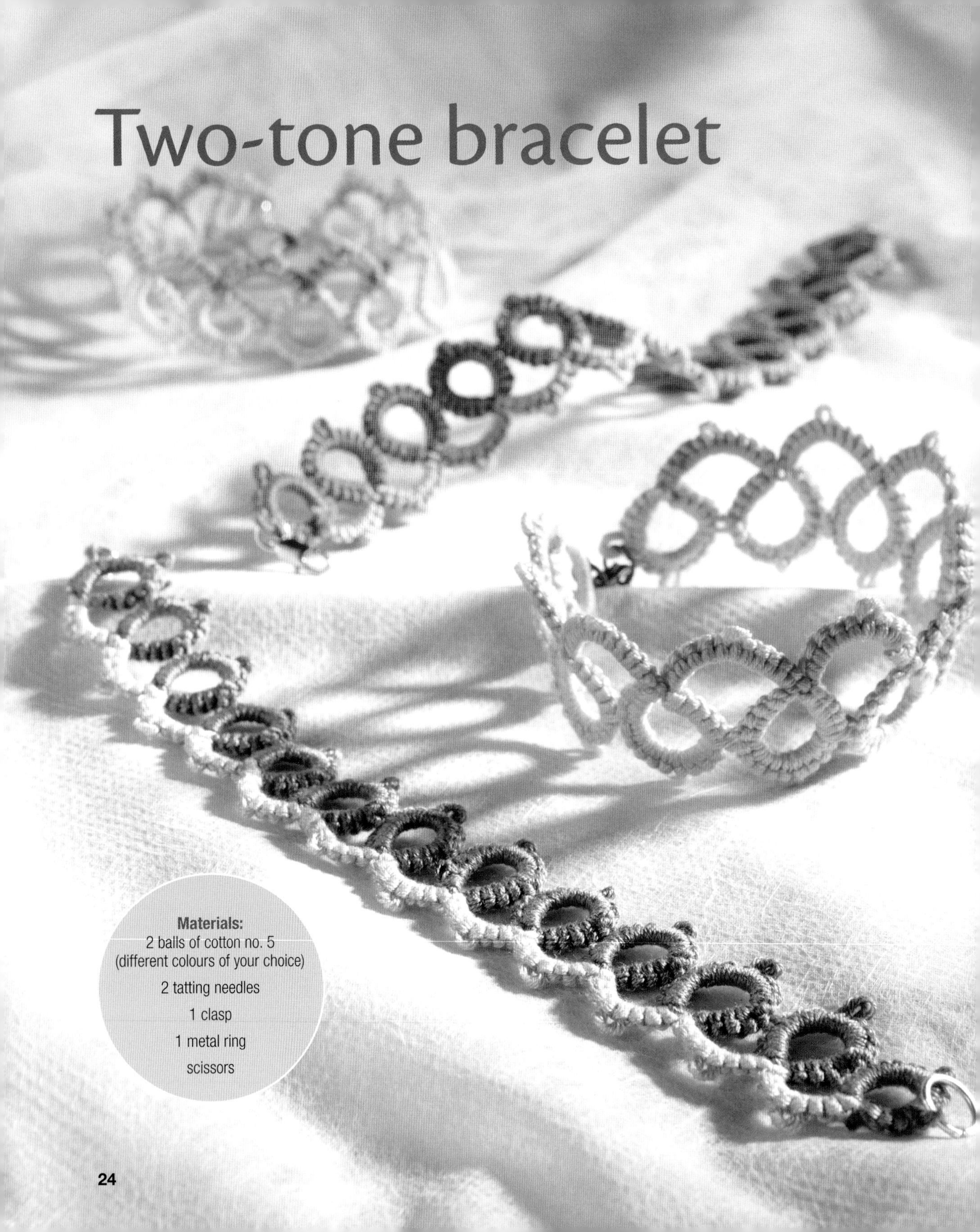

Materials:
2 balls of cotton no. 5
(different colours of your choice)

2 tatting needles

1 clasp

1 metal ring

scissors

1 Cut a length of about 2m (80in) of colour 1 from the ball of thread. You will use this for the rings. From the second ball, cut about 1.5m (60in) of thread. This is colour 2 and you will use it for the chain. Hold them together and make a slip knot in such a way that when the work is done, you will be able to open the knot. Thread a needle on to each of the two threads.

2 On the needle threaded with colour 2, using colour 1 make 5 double stitches and 1 picot three times. End with 5 more double stitches. Pull the thread through and close the ring. Turn the work over.

3–4 Now use the needle that is threaded with colour 1. On this needle, make 4 double stitches, 1 picot and 4 more double stitches. Pull the thread on the needle through the stitches so that they lie close together. Now you have a ring of one colour and a chain of the other colour. In this way the colour changes are not visible.

5 Continue to work, continuing to exchange needles: repeat the first step, but after the first 5 double stitches, pass the needle through a picot on the first ring. Make another two sequences with 5 double stitches and 1 picot and then end with 5 double stitches. Pull the thread through and close the ring.

6 Repeat steps 3–5 continuing to switch colours as explained above. The picture shows a detail of the finished work.

Spiral necklace

Materials:
1 ball of no. 5 thread
20 resin rose beads
1 tatting needle
1 needle to thread the rose beads
scissors, 1 clasp
and 1 metal jump ring

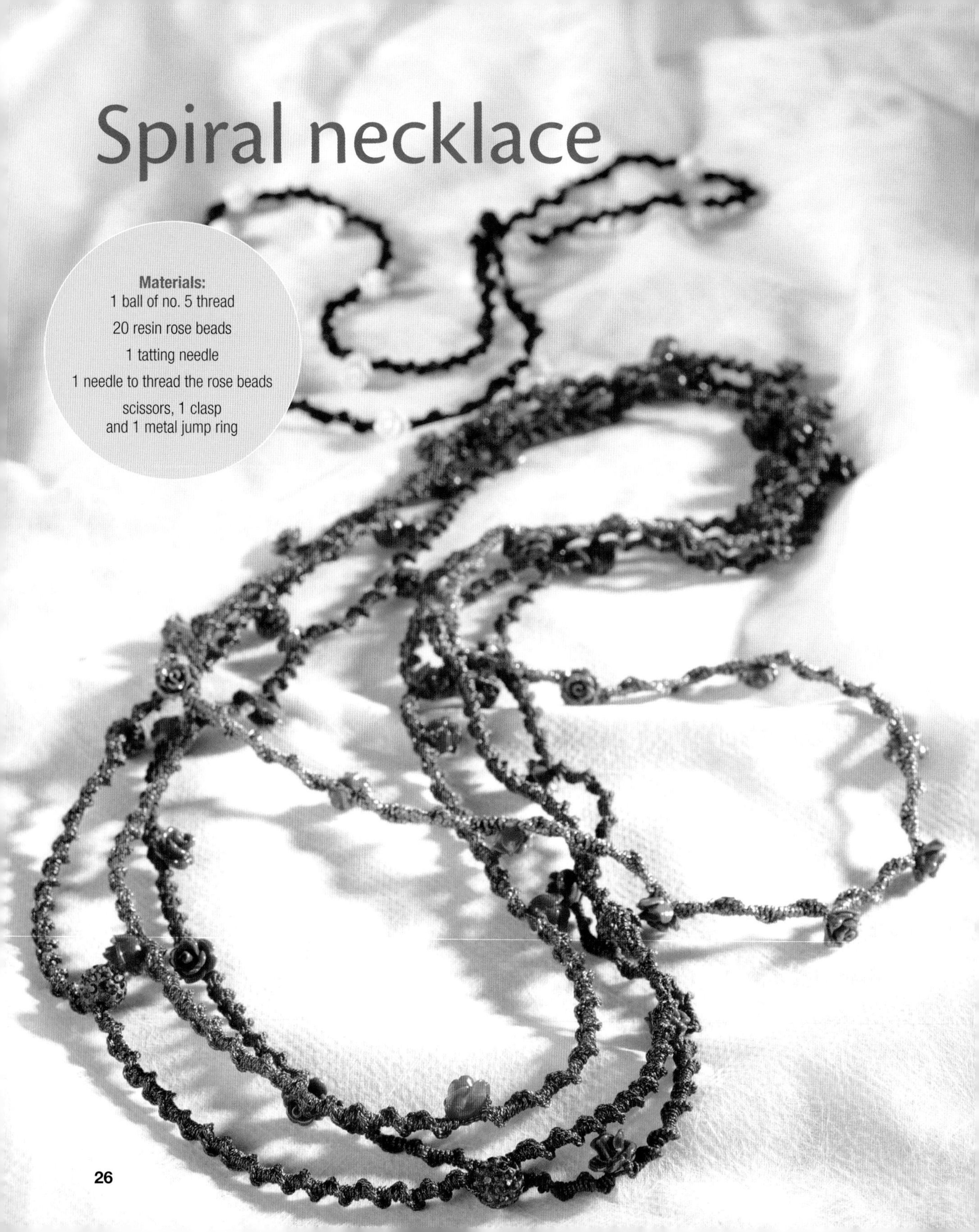

For this new technique, we will look at a simple design for some fashionable necklaces. This is something suitable for both experts and beginners alike, including children. You can use practically any type of thread – linen, cotton or laminated yarn. The final look will depend on the material you use.

1 Slide the rose beads and the clasp on the thread so that you can slip them up when you need them. Then thread the needle, leaving about 1m (40in) of thread free.

2 Make 2 double stitches. Slip the clasp close to the first stitches and make 2 more double stitches. Pull the needle through the ring and close it with a single knot. You have made the closure for your necklace.

3–4 Make a series of A or B half stitches. Because these stitches will all be on the same side, they will tend to twist to form a spiral. Follow the direction of the spiral and turn the work around the needle. Continue working and insert a flower bead, until the needle is full of stitches.

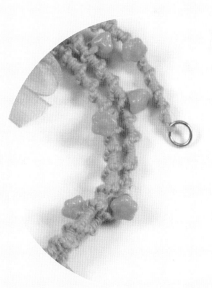

5–6 Now pull the needle and thread through the stitches. Continue, inserting another rose bead close to the last stitch. Make a new series of stitches and insert rose beads wherever you like. Work until your necklace is as long as you want. Finally, insert the metal jump ring, make a few knots to fix it in place and then pull the ends of the thread inside the spiral stitches of the necklace.

7 Detail of the finished work.

Rose place holders

Materials:
no. 5 thread in different colours:
green, yellow, fuchsia and orange
1 medium needle for tatting
1 glass bead for each
flower (optional)
1 crochet hook

 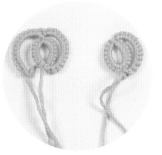 

1 To make the petals, start with the smallest one. Make 9 double stitches, 1 picot and 9 more double stitches. Pull the needle through the stitches, and tighten the thread to pull them together. Close the ring you have just made with a single knot. Remember to work with a continuous thread, so don't cut it.

2 Medium petal – turn the work on to the reverse, make 13 double stitches, pull the needle through them and let the work fall to the side that turns best. Close the chain that you have made, using the needle thread and join to the picot below (if you use the other thread it will make the work turn). Make 1 picot and 13 more double stitches. You will have another arch-shaped chain. Close this with a single knot at the base of the work.

3 Large petal: turn the work and make 17 double stitches. Pull the carrier thread through and compact the stitches. With the crochet hook, attach the chain to the picot below and make 17 more double stitches and close at the base with a double knot. Without cutting the thread, leave 0.5cm (¼in) of thread and make 8 more petals in the same way (repeat steps 1, 2 and 3).

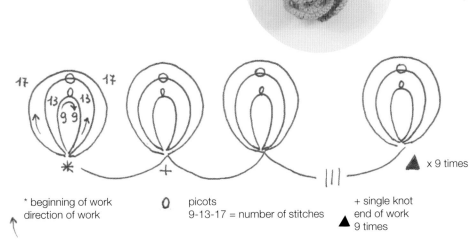

4 After you have made all the petals, pull them together to make a flower, shaping them with your fingers and stitching them together. Sew a bead into the centre.

x 9 times

* beginning of work
direction of work

0   picots
9-13-17 = number of stitches

+ single knot
end of work
9 times

Circle bracelet

Circle bracelet

Materials:
2 balls of no. 5 cotton, different colours

1 tatting needle

1 clasp

clear nail varnish and scissors

1 Thread the needle and leave 1m (40in) of thread hanging free. With the thread from the ball, make 10 double stitches and pull the needle through them with the carrier thread. Pull up slightly and slip the thread into the circle. Then close tightly by pulling both threads without making the final knot. This will form the closing ring of the bracelet.

2 Then, using the thread from the ball, make 7 double stitches.

Note:
With this technique, the work is done in two stages, using both the thread from the ball and the thread from the needle (if you decide to use the shuttle, you will need two shuttles). In order to work comfortably, the thread needs to be about four times the length of the finished item, plus 20cm (8in); the type and thickness (gauge) of the thread will also be a factor.

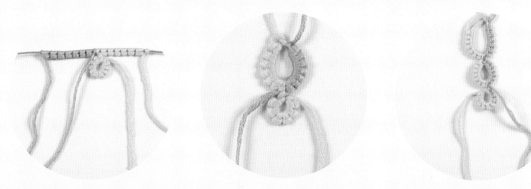

3 Now work on the eye side of the needle. Unthread the needle and work on the reverse of the work, using the other colour, making 7 double stitches. When you work on the reverse side of the work, start with a half stitch B and then make a half stitch A. Continue in this way and make the other double stitches.

4 Thread the needle again, draw it through the double stitches and then through the end loop. Pull the thread firmly.

5 Now use the other colour. Continue to work for the desired length, repeating steps 2, 3 and 4. When you have reached the end, insert the clasp and tie a closing knot. Apply a drop of clear nail varnish, pull the loose ends into the work for a few stitches and cut off the excess thread.

Variation:
When making two coloured circles working in opposite directions, you can use another method to insert the second coloured thread. After you have made the small starting loop and before you close it, insert the thread of the second colour leaving about 10cm (4in) out; then tighten the loop. This way the new thread is fixed in place. The leftover thread from the new colour (about 10cm, or 4in) and the starting thread from the first colour, left from the closure of the small loop, can be hidden when the project is completed.

6 Detail of the finished work.

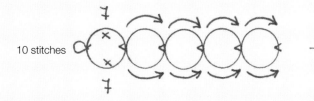

10 stitches

< = 2 threads
↻ direction of the work

X = number of double stitches according to your preference
——— length of the work

Bracelet with beads

Bracelet with beads

Materials:
1 ball of laminated thread

13 Swarovski spherical crystal beads with large central hole

1 clasp

1 needle for tatting

0.6mm crochet hook (USA size 10, UK size 4)

scissors

1 safety pin

This bracelet is made in the same way as the previous one, except that beads are inserted in the centre of the rings of double stitches.

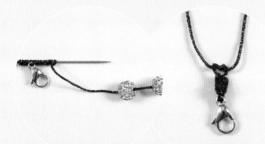

1–2 Slide on the clasp, the 13 beads and then the needle on to the working thread, leaving a free end of about 1m (40in). Make 4 double stitches, slide the clasp up to the stitches and make 4 more double stitches. Pull the needle through the stitches and pass it through the end loop. Close with a single knot. This is the closure for your bracelet.

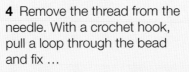

3 With the thread from the ball, make 10 double stitches.

4 Remove the thread from the needle. With a crochet hook, pull a loop through the bead and fix …

5 … a safety pin to the top. Pull the extra thread through, leaving a small loop.

6–7 Turn the work over. With the thread coming from the base of the bead make one B half stitch and then one A half stitch. Then make 9 double stitches on the eye side of the needle. Thread the needle with the carrier thread again and pass it through all 20 stitches. Pull the thread and tighten all the stitches. Remove the safety pin from the top of the bead and pick up the small loop with the needle and then insert it in the closing loop to the right. Pull the thread and close the ring, enclosing the bead and without making any knots.

8 Repeat steps 3–7 until the work is finished. Then make a small closing loop with 8 double stitches making a closed ring to attach the clasp.

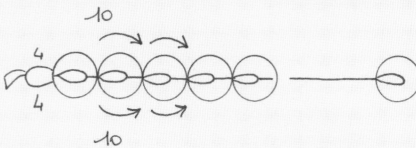

9 Detail of the finished work.

4–10 = number of stitches   ◯ insertion of bead

⤳ direction of work

Interwoven
bracelet

Materials:
2 balls of any thread of your
preference in contrasting colours

2 tatting needles

1 snap fastener or 1 clasp

The working technique is exactly like the one for the previous bracelet, except this one is done in two stages and with two balls of thread. It takes a fair amount of time, but the result is very eye-catching.

We will call these colours 1 and 2. They can even be of different materials, because they are two separate chains that start and end independently.

1 Thread a needle with colour 1 yarn. Leave 2m (80in) of thread free. Make 16 double stitches, pull the carrier thread through and close the ring with a single knot. Thread the second needle with colour 2 and make another ring just like the first. Before you close the ring, pass the two threads of the first ring through the second one, then pull the thread and close the second ring with a single knot.

2 With colour 1, make 8 double stitches, remove the needle from the thread and from the reverse of the work, make 8 double stitches starting with the B half stitch on the eye side of the needle. Pass the threads of colour 2 inside the ring before you pull the threads to close it. Thread the needle again and pull it through the stitches. Close the ring with a single knot.

3 Repeat the sequence in step 2 exchanging colours. Continue, repeating steps 1 and 2 until you reach the desired length.

4 Detail of the finished work.

Daisy bracelet

Daisy bracelet

Materials:
1 ball of cotton no. 10

1 tatting needle

1 crochet hook

1 clasp and 1 metal jump ring

contrasting coloured
service thread

1 Thread the needle and leave about 50cm (20in) of thread in the eye. Make 2 double stitches and 1 picot, seven times all together. Close with 2 double stitches.

2 Pull the thread through the stitches and close the ring. Make a single knot at the end.

3 Now start the chains. Insert a service thread inside the first stitches (see technique on page 20). Make 7 double stitches, 1 picot and 7 double stitches. Then pull the needle through the stitches and pull lightly to compact them. Skip the picot right after the closure of the base ring and go to the second picot and, with the help of the crochet hook, pull out a loop and pass the needle through it to close the first chain.

4 Work the remaining 3 chains in the same way.

5–6 While making the last chain, use the service thread (see technique on page 20). When the chain is complete, end the work with a single knot. Hide the loose thread ends.

7 Make another motif. Make the first 2 chains and then 7 double stitches. With the help of the crochet hook pull a loop out through the picot in the finished motif and slide the needle through it. Make a B half stitch, continue as usual and finish the chain. Repeat for the last chain. Make as many motifs as you need to reach the desired length and finish with a double knot. For the final fastening loop, use the end threads. Make 15 double stitches and close the loop with a knot. Fix a metal jump ring on the chain at one end of the bracelet and on the other, fix the clasp.

8 Detail of the finished work.

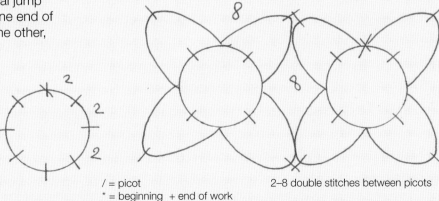

/ = picot
* = beginning + end of work

2–8 double stitches between picots

Square earrings with Swarovski crystals

Square earrings with Swarovski crystals

Materials:
1 ball of no. 10 cotton

40 Swarovski crystal beads diameter 6mm (¼in)

2 earring hooks

1 tatting needle

1 beading needle

1m (40in) of no. 30 silver plated wire

1 crochet hook

1 Using the beading needle, string 5 beads on to the thread. Then thread the tatting needle, leaving about 50cm (20in) of thread in the eye. Make 2 double stitches, then slide 1 bead up and make 2 more double stitches and 1 picot, three times in total. End with 2 double stitches, 1 bead and 2 double stitches. Then pull the needle through the stitches, insert the needle in the final loop and pull the carrier thread to form a ring. Close the ring with a single knot.

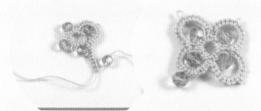

2–3 Make the chains: make 8 double stitches, 1 picot and 8 double stitches. Pull the needle through the stitches and pull lightly to compact the stitches. Go around the crystal bead and pull out a loop from the next picot with the help of the crochet hook. Next, thread the needle with the carrier thread, pull the thread and block the chain in position above the crystal bead. Make the next chain as just described, but in place of the picot, insert the fifth crystal bead. Complete the flower with 2 more chains like the first one, and end the last one with a double knot. We will be making 3 more flowers like this one.

4–5 For the second flower, first follow step 1 above. Make the first 2 chains exactly as described in step 2. For the third chain, after the first 8 double stitches, attach it to the first flower by pulling a loop out of the picot of the chain just before the fifth crystal bead. Make 8 more double stitches and close the chain. For the fourth chain, after making 8 double stitches, pull another loop through the picot of the next chain on the first flower, diagonally opposite to the fifth bead on the motif. Make 8 double stitches and close the chain. You have finished the second flower: you now have two flowers joined together.

6–7–8 Start the third flower as previously described. On the third chain, after 8 double stitches, pull a loop through the picot of the first chain of the first flower, the one just before the external crystal. Pass the needle through it, make 8 double stitches, go around the crystal bead and fasten the flower to the next picot. Proceed with the fourth chain: make 8 double stitches, pull a loop through the second picot (of the first flower, the one where the first and second flowers are already joined together, or the picot that will be at the centre of the four flowers), make 8 double stitches, go around the crystal bead and end.

9–10 Start the fourth flower as described in step 1. While you are making the first chain, join it to the free picot of the second flower. Continue, making the second chain with the crystal bead, the third chain joined to the free picot of the third flower and, finally, the fourth chain which you will join to the central picot where the other three flowers are already joined together. At the end of this work, cut off a length of silver wire, pass it through one of the external crystal beads and attach an earring hook.

CENTRAL SECTION

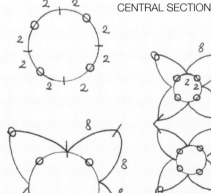

1 complete flower

O = bead
/ = picot
2–8 double stitches

Flower earrings

Flower earrings

Materials:

1 ball of no. 5 cotton

2 silver earring hooks

2 Swarovski crystal beads and 8 crystal bicone beads

2 silver head pins

2 open jump rings

2 mountings with Swarovski crystals

1 tatting needle

1 crochet hook

1 pair of wire cutters

1 pair of round-nosed pliers

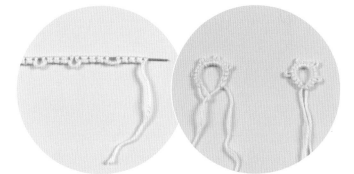

1–2 Thread the needle, leaving 1.5m (60in) of thread in the eye of the needle. With the thread from the ball, make 4 double stitches and 1 picot, four times in all. End with 4 double stitches, pull the thread through the stitches, pass the needle through the end loop and close the ring, pulling the threads firmly.

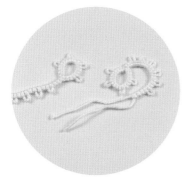 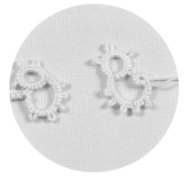 

3 With the thread from the ball, make 4 double stitches and 1 picot. Make 3 double stitches and 1 picot, four times in all and end with 4 double stitches.

4 Make 4 double stitches with the thread from the ball. Turn the work. With the crochet hook pull a loop out through the picot of the base ring and pass the needle through it. Make one B half stitch, then 4 double stitches. Pull the thread through the stitches. You have now made the first petal.

5 Repeat the two previous steps four times. At the end, tie off the threads leaving an open ring. Make a pendant by inserting the crystal bead and 4 beads on the head pin. With the round-nosed pliers, make a small ring at the end of the pin (cut off the excess length with the wire cutter) and hook it to the jump ring that you have already inserted. Sew the mounted crystal to the centre and attach the earring hook to the picot on the opposite side to the crystal pendant. Repeat to make the second earring.

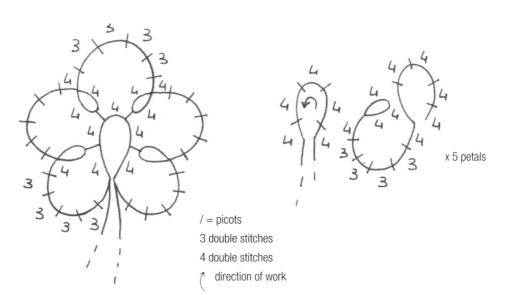

x 5 petals

/ = picots

3 double stitches

4 double stitches

↻ direction of work

Four-leaf clover bracelet

Four-leaf clover bracelet

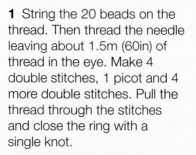

1 String the 20 beads on the thread. Then thread the needle leaving about 1.5m (60in) of thread in the eye. Make 4 double stitches, 1 picot and 4 more double stitches. Pull the thread through the stitches and close the ring with a single knot.

2 Slide a bead down next to the ring and then make 8 double stitches. Pass the thread through the stitches, make a single knot and slide down another bead.

3 Make 6 double stitches, pull a loop through the previous picot and pass the needle through it, make 6 double stitches and pull the thread through the stitches. Close the ring with a single knot and slide down a bead.

4 Turn the work. Make 16 double stitches, then make a single knot and slide a bead down the string. Make 6 stitches, pull a loop through the picot of the previous petal and put the needle through it. Then pull the thread, make 6 double stitches, pull the thread again and close the ring with a knot.

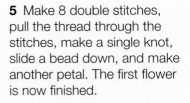

5 Make 8 double stitches, pull the thread through the stitches, make a single knot, slide a bead down, and make another petal. The first flower is now finished.

6 Repeat step 5. Now work on only one side until the bracelet is the desired length. Continue to make only half of the clovers and chains. When you reach the end, make 4 double stitches, slip on the clasp and make 4 more double stitches. Then make a single knot, slide down a bead and continue with the steps to complete the other side. Tie and hide the threads, and when the work is completed, cut off the loose ends and give these knots a light coat of clear nail varnish.

7 Detail of the finished work.

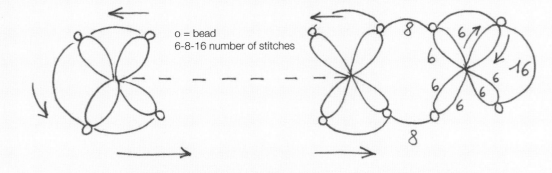

o = bead
6-8-16 number of stitches

Necklace
and earrings
with roses

Necklace and earrings with roses

Materials:
1 spool of metallic blue thread
1 spool of metallic lilac thread
9 beads with lilac-coloured crystals
5 blue beads
1 clasp
2 earring hooks
1 tatting needle
clear nail varnish
scissors

Note:
For this work it is preferable to use short lengths of thread in the needle as the metallic thread can be damaged by passing it through the eye. If necessary, change the thread by inserting new lengths at the end of the leaves or the chains using the technique described on page 19.

1 Thread the needle leaving about 1m (40in) of free thread. Make 8 double stitches, pull the thread through, pass the needle through the loop and pull the stitches. Make a chain of 10 double stitches, pull the thread lightly and make a single knot.

2 Make 1 leaf with 8 double stitches, 1 picot and 8 double stitches. Pull the thread through, make a single knot at the base and make another leaf next to the first one.

3 Continue, making chains and leaves for about 20cm (8in). Remember that the chains are worked on the reverse of the work.

4 Make a new chain with 2 leaves. Tie a single knot, insert a blue bead on one of the two threads and fix it in place with a knot on the reverse of the work. Make 1 chain and close it with a knot.

5 To make the rose, thread the needle with the lilac thread, leaving about 1m (40in) in the eye. Insert this between the stitches on the chain and tie the two threads together with a knot at the base of the chain. Leave free and uncut the ends of the blue thread that you have been working with until now. Start working and make 6 double stitches, 1 picot, 12 double stitches, 1 picot and 6 double stitches. Pull the thread and close the ring. You have made the first petal. Make 6 double stitches and, with the help of the crochet hook, pull a loop through the first picot of the previous petal. Continue the work and finish the second petal. In the same way, make 2 more petals.

6 Without separating the layers, make another round of petals. Each petal is made of 5 double stitches, 1 picot, 10 double stitches, 1 picot and 5 double stitches. Create 2 more petals as just described. At the end of this round, insert a lilac bead at the centre and fix it with the carrier thread. Cut it at the back of the work. Continue to work on the necklace, once again picking up the blue threads (left aside), alternating chains, leaves and flowers until you reach the desired length.

7 Use the same technique to make the earrings. Remember to protect all the joins with clear nail varnish after cutting off the excess thread.

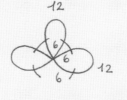

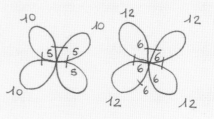

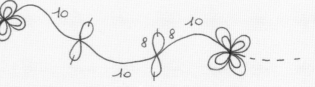

Purse and
mobile phone pouch

Purse

Materials:

3 balls of pink Anchor metallic thread

1 purse frame with a 10cm (4in) wide base

1 tatting needle

30cm (12in) of lining in a matching colour

2mm (UK size 14, US size 0) crochet hook

sewing thread matching the metallic thread above

tailor's chalk

pins

scissors

sewing needle

metal chain 70cm (28in) long

1 Thread the needle with the metallic thread, leaving 1m (40in) of thread on the needle. Make 5 double stitches and 1 picot on the pointed side of the needle, repeat, then make 2 double stitches and 1 picot, five times in all. End with 2 double stitches. Pull the thread through the stitches and make a single knot at the base.

2 Turn the work and make a chain starting with 3 double stitches. Then make 1 picot and 2 double stitches, seven times in all. Then make 1 double stitch, pull the thread through the stitches and make a single knot. Pull out a loop through the central picot of the previous ring and pass the needle through it.

3 Repeat steps 1 and 2, five more times: you have completed the first row. Turn the work over, make 6 double stitches, 1 picot and 6 double stitches. Then make a single knot: you have made the connecting chain for the second row. Continue working as explained in steps 1 and 2, until you have 7 completed motifs (the central part of the purse). When you are making the 7 motifs, take care to attach the picots on the chains to each other where the two rows join each other, using the technique of pulling the loop through the picots (see page 18, 'Joining motifs').

4 Make the central section of both sides of the purse as explained above. Then on both sides work a complete round of chains using your crochet hook (1 US single crochet, 3 chains and 1 single crochet/UK double crochet, 3 chains, double crochet), hooking on to the picots below to give the work a uniform look. After this, work another round of single crochet (UK double crochet).

5 Make a strip with a width of 4 double crochet (UK treble crochet) stitches, and as long as necessary to make a border to finish the front of the purse. When this is done, join the stitches. Sew the border to the row of single crochet (UK double crochet) stitches starting from the centre bottom part of the purse with small hidden stitches. Make another strip for the back of the purse and join it to the body in the same way.

6 Fitting the frame: position the frame above the handwork. Using a contrasting thread, mark the purse side openings. Work from the mark upwards making a round of chains in the following way: using the crochet hook make, on the border below, 1 single crochet (UK double crochet) and 10 chains. Skip 2 double crochets (UK treble crochets) and 1 single crochet (UK double crochet) for the entire length of the opening until you get to the mark on the other side. Make another series of chains and fill in the top part of the work. Repeat for the second half of the purse.

7–8 On only one side of the purse, starting from the edge of the frame and working downwards, until you reach the other side, make 1 single crochet (UK double crochet) and 10 chains. Then skip 2 double crochets (UK treble crochets) and 1 single crochet (UK double crochet). This way you have created a series of arches on the outside edge. Hold the two halves together (placing the second one on the first) and join them starting from the marked opening point and making: 1 single crochet (UK double crochet), 5 chains, 1 single crochet (UK double crochet) (on the centre of the arch you made on the other part of the purse), 5 chains, skip 2 double crochets (UK treble crochets) and make 1 single crochet (UK double crochet). Continue, repeating the sequence starting with 5 chains, until you reach the mark on the other side. This way you have joined the two parts of the purse.

Assembly
Fold the lining into two, place it above the work, pin it, and mark the outlines with tailor's chalk. Lift off the tatted work and cut the lining, leaving about 0.5cm (¼in) seam allowance. Sew the two parts of the lining together with invisible stitches and turn the work inside out. Fit the lining inside the purse and baste it in place. For a better fit you can make a small fold inside the lining at the hinge opening position. Stitch the purse and lining to the holes in the frame. Then remove the basting threads and sew together again. After this attach the chain.

Mobile phone pouch

1 Using the technique and stitches described above, make a tatted strip 26cm (10¼in) long and 9cm (3½in) wide. This work is made up of four rows of modules. At the end of the work, fold the strip in half and cut the lining as explained on page 63 (*see 'Assembly'*), and stitch the lining. Sew both sides of the work together with tiny invisible stitches. Leave 4cm (1½in) open at the top of each side for the frame opening. Fit the lining inside the tatted work and sew both parts to the frame.

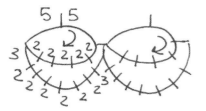

l = picot

direction of work

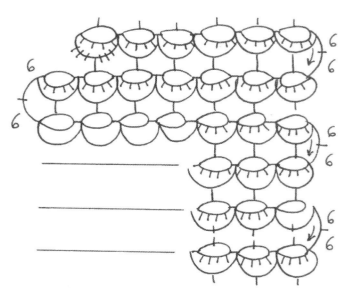

Necklace and earrings with ring motif

Lilac earrings

Materials:

1 spool of lilac metallic thread

2 lilac-coloured mounted Swarovski crystals

2 earring hooks

1 tatting needle

1 sewing needle

scissors

clear nail varnish

1 crochet hook

safety pin

1 Make a first ring with 5 double stitches and 1 picot, three times. End with 5 double stitches, pull the carrier thread through, insert the needle in the end loop and pull the thread lightly. Tie a single knot to end. Then make a second ring identical to the first.

2 Start the third ring: make 5 double stitches and, with the crochet hook, pull a loop from the picot of the first ring, using the spool thread. Pass the needle through the loop and through the second ring. Continue, making 5 double stitches and 1 picot, twice over. End with 5 double stitches. Pull the thread through and close the ring in such a way that the second ring is caught between the first and the third which are linked together. Make the fourth ring and link it to the second, with the third one between the two. Continue in this way until you have a total of 10 rings.

3–4 Now make the eleventh ring: make 5 double stitches and, with the help of the crochet hook, pull a loop through the picot of the ninth ring. Make 5 double stitches, 1 picot and 5 double stitches. Then pull the carrier thread and pull in the extra thread until you have a small loop that you will keep open with a safety pin. From the picot of the first (starting) ring, pull out a loop and pass the needle through it. Make 5 double stitches, pull the needle and thread through and then pass the needle through the loop (which is being kept open with the safety pin). Then remove the safety pin and pull the carrier thread firmly to compact the last ring that you made. End with a single knot.

5–6–7–8 For the twelfth ring, take the threads to the back of the work and make 5 double stitches. Using the crochet hook, pull a loop out of the picot on the second ring that you made, and pass the needle through it. Continue with 5 double stitches, 1 picot and 5 double stitches. Then pull the needle and thread through the stitches, bring the threads to the front and pull a loop through the picot on the eleventh ring. Finish with 5 double stitches, pull the carrier thread through and close the ring with a final knot.

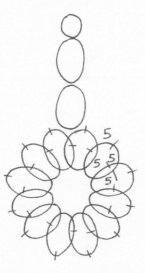

9–10 Pass the two threads through the work (invisibly) to the outside of the flower that you have created by assembling all 12 rings. Now make the rings that will join to the earring hook. Make 5 double stitches on the pointed side of the needle and 5 double stitches on the eye side. Thread the needle and pull the thread through. End with a single knot. Make a second ring like the first. Make a third ring, but smaller, with 3 + 3 double stitches. Close with a final knot, hide the threads inside the work, cut off the loose ends and fix them in place with clear nail varnish. Sew the mounted stone to the centre of the flower. Attach the earring hook.

You can also make pieces in alternating colours using the technique described above.

Grey necklace

Materials:
1 spool of charcoal grey metallic thread
3 grey crystal beads
60 6mm (¼in) crystal beads
1 clasp
1 closed jump ring
1 tatting needle
1 sewing needle
scissors and flat pliers
clear nail varnish
1 crochet hook
no. 25 nylon thread
metal crimp beads

Make the first flower using the same procedure as the earrings. When you are making the second one, before you finish the last two rings (eleventh and twelfth rings), using the outer picots, hook them to the completed first flower. Make a third flower and join it to the first and second ones following the technique described on page 18 ('Joining motifs').

For the back part of the necklace, cut two pieces of nylon thread, pass them through the fourth picot of flowers 1 and 2, counting from the picot where they are attached to each other, on the top part of the flowers. Fix one end of the nylon thread with a crimp bead. Thread 30 crystal beads onto the string, then the crimp bead and the clasp. Pass the thread through the crimp bead again and with a pair of flat pliers, squeeze it closed. Repeat for the other side of the necklace inserting the jump ring.

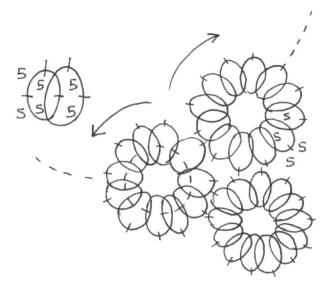

Blue earrings

Materials:
1 spool of metallic blue thread

6 blue crystal beads

2 earring hooks

1 tatting needle

1 sewing needle

scissors

clear nail varnish

1 crochet hook

1–2–3–4 Make the first flower as described for the lilac earrings. For the second flower, make a base circle with 1 double stitch and 1 very small picot, six times in all. End with 6 double stitches, pull the thread through and close with a single knot. Continue to work on the second flower, made up of only 6 rings, as described for the lilac flower but with the difference that every ring is closed on the base ring picot. This means that, before pulling out the loop to close the ring, the needle passes through the small picot that you made on the base ring. With the fifth ring, during the last part (instead of the third picot), use your crochet hook to pull out a loop from the outer picot of any ring in the finished flower and pass the needle through. End with 5 double stitches and close the ring on the base ring. The sixth ring is the last one. Start as with the fifth ring but join it to the finished flower on the previous ring. Using the same method as you used for this half flower, make the third part (half flower) to complete the earring. Work on the front. You will have a half flower identical to the first but facing the other way. Sew the three beads to the centre of the flowers and attach the earring hooks.

Clover necklace

Clover necklace

Materials:
14 grey crystal bicone beads
1 spool of grey metallic thread
1 tatting needle
1 clasp
2 jump rings, one closed and one open
1 beading needle

1 Using the beading needle, string the beads on the spool thread and let them slide up the thread. Now thread the tatting needle, and leave 2m (80in) of thread free. To make the end fastening ring, make 10 double stitches, pull the needle and carrier thread through the stitches and close with a single knot, making a ring.

2 Make 14 double stitches, pull the thread and close making a loop. Make another one just like it, then make a third one with 7 double stitches, 1 picot and 7 double stitches. Pull the thread through and close the ring.

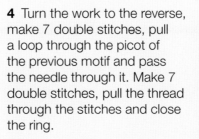

3 Turn the work to the reverse, make a chain with 14 double stitches, pull the thread through and close with a single knot.

4 Turn the work to the reverse, make 7 double stitches, pull a loop through the picot of the previous motif and pass the needle through it. Make 7 double stitches, pull the thread through the stitches and close the ring.

5 Slide a crystal bead down to the base of the thread. Make 2 rings of 14 double stitches each. Continue in this way until you have reached the length you prefer, making rings and chains and inserting the crystal beads following the instructions given above, repeating steps 2 to 5.

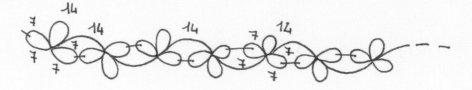

Purple and fuchsia collar

Materials:

4 skeins of purple stranded cotton (embroidery floss)

4 skeins of fuchsia stranded cotton (embroidery floss)

10 fuchsia beads with Swarovski crystals

30 fuchsia bicone crystal beads

5 purple crystal beads

1 clasp

1 jump ring

1 tatting needle

1 sewing needle

4 crimp beads

no. 25 nylon thread

1 crochet hook

1 Make a ring by repeating 2 double stitches and 1 picot, a total of 13 times; then make 2 double stitches. When this is done, pull the thread through the stitches and close the ring.

2 On this base ring, make 6 double stitches, 1 picot and 6 more double stitches. Skipping one base ring picot, pull a loop through the next picot with a crochet hook and pass the needle through it. Repeat this six more times. Then make a final closing knot. You have now made the first motif of the collar.

3 Continue to work following the diagram. Join the motifs together using the picots. When you have reached the end, sew the 10 crystal beads inside the small flowers and the 5 purple crystal beads between the large flowers. With the 30 fuchsia-coloured crystal beads make the back part of the necklace, using nylon thread and crimp beads as described on page 70.

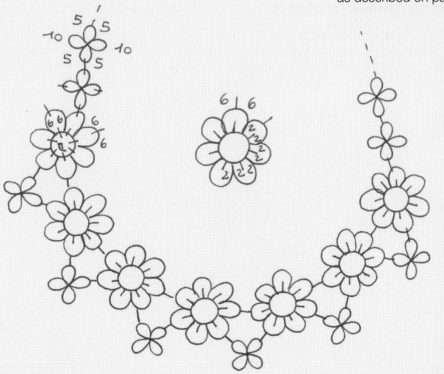

Beaded favours

Beaded favours

Materials:
1 ball of pink no. 10 cotton
1 box of Miyuki glass seed beads, colour coordinated with the thread
1 beading needle
1 tatting needle
1 crochet hook

Thread the beads on to the pink thread using the beading needle. Slide them up the thread close to the ball.

1 Thread the tatting needle leaving about 50cm (20) of thread on the other side of the needle. Make 5 double stitches, 1 picot and 4 double stitches. Slide 5 beads close to the needle against the last stitch (they will determine the picot length) and make 1 picot with the beads, then 4 double stitches, 1 picot and 5 double stitches. Close to obtain the base ring. End with a single knot.

2 Turn the work over, make 3 double stitches and 1 picot with beads, seven times in all. Then make 3 double stitches, and when this is done, pull the thread through the stitches. Then make a single knot. This is the first chain.

3 Next make 5 double stitches.
With the crochet hook pull a loop through the picot of the first base ring and pass the needle through it. Continue, making 4 double stitches, 1 picot with beads, 4 double stitches, 1 picot and 5 double stitches. You have now finished the second base ring.

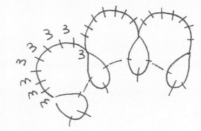

Following the diagrams, make the second row of petals with 6 base rings and 6 chains and then the third one with 4 base circles and 3 chains closing the last one as described above. To assemble the flower, set the second row of petals into the centre of the first and stitch together with small stitches. Finally fix the smallest row of petals inside the flower, after moulding the petals into a curved shape. Fix well and hide the thread ends. Shape the petals so that they look harmonious.

4 Continue to work as described in steps 1, 2 and 3. Make a total of 8 base rings and 8 external chains. End by joining the last chain to the base, through the only remaining free picot on the first base ring. Finish this circle with the last chain joined to the base where the first one started. Join and hide the thread ends. Pass a thread through the beaded picots on the base ring and pull the two ends of this thread, closing and gathering the centre of this flower.

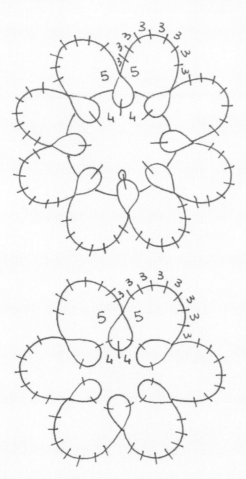

I = picots
4-5-3 = stitches between picots

Sachets with poinsettias

The poinsettias

Materials:
1 ball of red silk
crochet thread

1 gilded bead

1 tatting needle

1 ball of no. 40 craft wire

florist's stem tape

1 flexible metal rod

round-nosed pliers

wire cutter

1 Thread the needle leaving at least 1m (40in) of thread free. Make 8 double stitches. Then make 1 picot and 2 double stitches, three times in all. Complete with 6 double stitches. Pull the needle through, form the ring and make a knot at the base. Do not cut the thread.

2 Make another ring starting with 11 double stitches. Then make 1 picot and 2 double stitches, three times in all, and finish with 9 double stitches. Pull the needle through, and make a knot at the base without cutting the thread.

3 Make a third ring starting with 11 double stitches. Then make 1 picot and 2 double stitches, four times in all. Complete with 9 double stitches. Pull the needle through, close the ring and make a knot at the base. Now cut the thread leaving about 10cm (4in) hanging.

4 As described in steps 1, 2 and 3 above, make 4 more bunches of 3 rings apiece.

5 Cut off a 20cm (8in) length of craft wire, thread the bead onto it and fold it in half, twisting it to block the bead in place at the base. Cut the metal rod to 15cm (6in) to make a stem and fix the bead and the first group of 3 rings on the stem. Wind the wire around the stem and fix the three parts firmly.

6 Using the craft wire, position the remaining 4 bunches of rings around the stem and fix them in place, moulding the petals so that they look balanced. Finally, cover the stem with florist's stem tape. Using the round-nosed pliers, twist it into a graceful spiral.

The sachets

Patterns for sachets on which the poinsettias are applied.

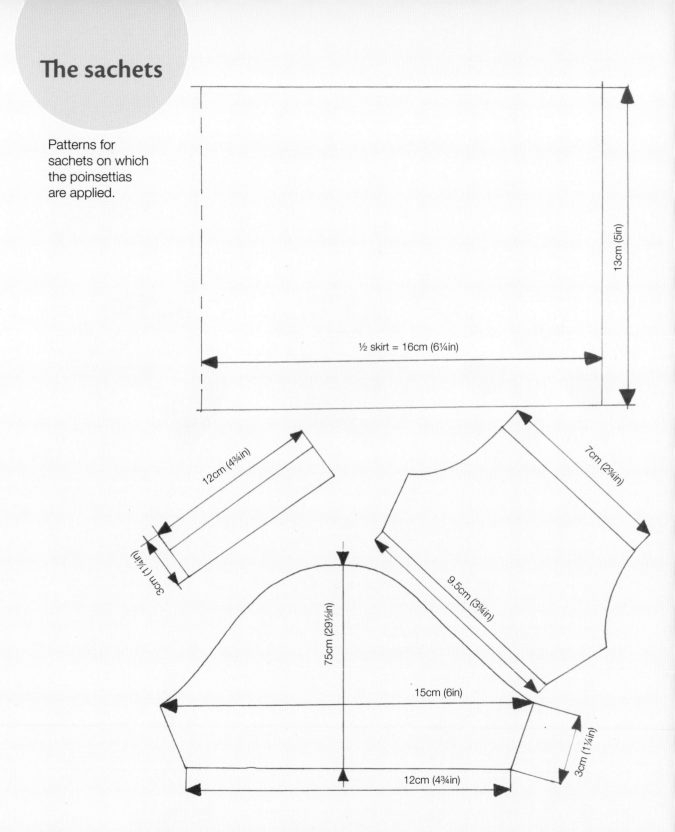

13cm (5in)

½ skirt = 16cm (6¼in)

12cm (4¾in)

3cm (1¼in)

7cm (2¾in)

9.5cm (3¾in)

75cm (29½in)

15cm (6in)

3cm (1¼in)

12cm (4¾in)

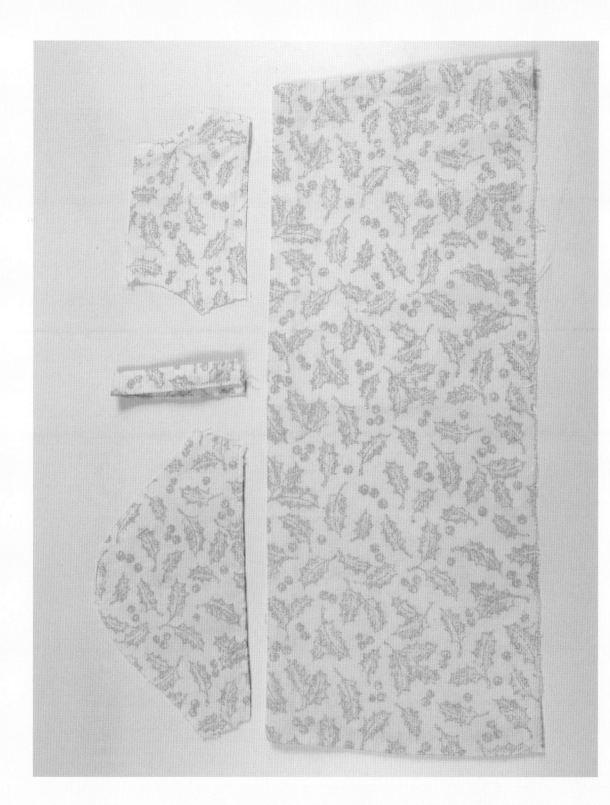

Flowers

Materials:
2 balls of no. 5 cotton
in pink and green

1 flexible metal rod
40cm (16in) long

florist's stem tape

no. 40 craft wire

1 tatting needle

1–2 Thread the needle with pink thread, leaving a tail of about 1m (40in) and make 7 double stitches. Continue, making 1 picot and 2 double stitches, repeated seven times. Then make 5 double stitches, pass the needle though, close the ring and tie a single knot. Without cutting the thread make 4 more rings, then cut the thread leaving about 10cm (4in). Make 2 more bunches of 5 rings each in the same way.

3 Thread the needle with green thread and make two pairs of leaves. Make 4 double stitches. Then make a picot and 2 double stitches, three times in all. Then make 2 double stitches, pull the needle through, close the ring and tie a single knot. Continue without cutting the thread and make 5 double stitches. Then make 1 picot and 2 double stitches, five times in all. Finally, make 3 double stitches. Repeat these two motifs once more.

4 To put them together, gather the 3 bunches of pink rings and set them on the top end of the rod. Using a piece of craft wire, closely wind the 6 thread ends from the 3 bunches around the rod and fix them tightly, twisting the threads together. Using the florist's stem tape, cover the stem and insert the two pairs of green leaves.

Black choker

Materials:
1 ball of black metallic thread
1m (40in) of black organza ribbon
1 tatting needle
5 mounted black Swarovski crystals
5 grey iron-on crystals
5 black iron-on crystals
1 sewing needle

1 Thread the needle and make the first petal: make 6 double stitches, 1 picot and 6 double stitches, then pull the needle and carrier thread through them. Close the petal in a ring passing the thread through the loop. Tie a single knot. Repeat this two more times to make a total of 3 petals.

2 Turn the work, make 6 double stitches and 1 picot, repeat. Then make 3 double stitches, pass the needle with the carrier thread through the stitches and make a single knot to close the first chain.

3 Turn the work, make 3 double stitches, 1 picot and 3 double stitches. Pull a loop through the picot on the adjacent petal and pass the needle through it. Then continue with 3 double stitches and 1 picot, three times in all. End with 3 double stitches. Pull the thread and close the loop. Turn the work and make a second chain: make 3 double stitches, 1 picot, 6 double stitches, 1 picot and 6 double stitches. Finish with a single knot. Make a petal as described in step 1 and join it, using a loop pulled through the fourth picot of the adjacent ring.

4 Finish as in step 1 making 2 more petals. Continue with 6 double stitches, pulling a loop through the picot of the previous chain, make 6 double stitches, 1 picot and 3 double stitches. You have now finished a sequence of modules.

5 Repeat steps 3 and 4, until you reach the desired length. End the work with the module you obtained in step 1 (so that the first and last modules are identical). End the work with a double knot. Cut the threads. Make the bottom half in the same way as the top, joining the halves at the picots on the chains. Hide the thread ends.

6 In the centre of the choker, sew the five mounted crystals and, if desired, iron on the two colours of crystals.

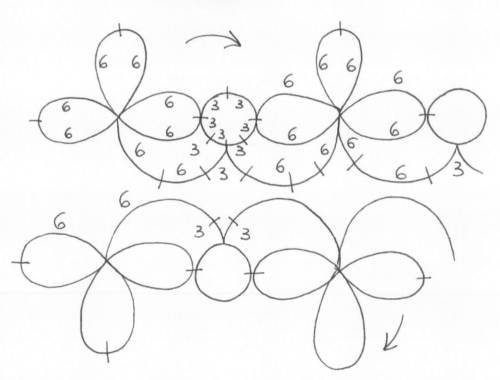

Detail of the necklace.

When you've really got the hang of tatted lace, this beautiful tatted vest is an example of the type of charming piece you could make for yourself!